Dedicated to my lil' sister Marsha who always knew that love, laughter, family, tea and a Clark Bar were life's sweetest treasures.

Acknowledgements

Our thanks to the many, many candy makers, candy companies, and candy stores that make our world a lil' sweeter. To our illustrator, Sergio Drumond, for his amazing illustrations, setting the book up and his endless patience with our edits. Debra would like to give shout out to Thanh who brought lots of sass even though, for shame, she's not a candy lover. To members of the candy team who helped compile candy information including Jeff Numero and Portia Alexander Ross. To my family and friends who did the obligatory oohs and aahs when reading drafts of this book. And finally, to my husband, Bill Balint for his edits after reading multiple versions of this book many, many times.

A Lil' Twirly Story of Candy

Purple Owl Publishing
Newton, MA 02461
Copyright 2019
Follow us on Facebook @lilcandystores

Table of Contents

Introduction

Introduction

Sometimes I think that the one thing I love most about being an adult is the right to buy candy whenever and wherever I want. - Ryan Gosling [2011, Aug. 9 Interview with Esquire]

We started this candy journey with a simple question: Where is the birthplace of candy in the United States? Much to our surprise, we were unable to find an answer. As we traveled down candy lane, seemingly simple questions led to mystery, intrigue and drama.

- When did chocolate become a candy?
- Who made the first lollipop in the US?
- How and when did sugar become so villainized?

Each time we thought we had found the answers, contradictory accounts surfaced from a Pandora's box of candy folklore.Before long, we were so overwhelmed with stories that we were unable to distinguish candy fact from candy fiction.

The further we dug for answers, the more questions emerged: what is candy? Is chocolate candy? Is candy when you add sugar to something? Is candy when you boil sugar? Why are cakes not candy? What's the difference between desserts, sweets and candy? Why is this so confusing?

We thus tell the twisting, twirling, and tasty story of candy hoping that future confectionery detectives will be spared tireless months of candy research. Our story features candy innovators as creative as Disney, candy makers as unusual and interesting as any Willy Wonka character, candy naming as frivolous as designer baby clothes, candy tales as ironic as that of dynamite inventor, Alfred Nobel, winner of the 1930 Nobel Peace Prize, candy feuds as scandalous as Watergate, and candy takeovers as dramatic and gripping as *Hunger Games*.

This little story begins by defining what is candy, exploring the ancient past (okay, maybe not ancient *ancient* but 17th century ancient) of sweet delectables--and delving into the good, the bad, and the sweet--within the candy world, from the cane fields to the candy store. Our second chapter explores the birthplace of candy in the US, leading us through more twists and turns within the world of candy. Next, we examine the bitter passages of chocolate's liquid beginnings to present day cacao controversies. We "slap" our way through the history of lollipops in our fourth chapter (you'll see what we mean later).

Our chewy fifth chapter explores the not so edible (but delicious) story of gums (and no we don't mean the gum in your teeth) and its run in with trees, chalk, oil, petroleum, and so forth (you know you're curious). We end with the lessons learned on the joys and horrors that make candy's history all the more bitter, sweet, and tasty.

Each chapter includes pictures, trivia, recipes, and maps. As we wrote this book, we shook our heads and laughed a lot; we wondered and were amazed at the hype, folklore and deep love and passion of confectioners; and of course we had to stop many times to get something sweet to eat. Grab a few *cough* dozen) sweets and join us as we tell a little twirly story of candy.

Chapter 1

Opening Pandora's sweet box

I went to the bank and asked to borrow a cup of money. They said, 'What for?' I said, 'I'm going to buy some sugar.' -- *Comedian, Steven Wright*

What is candy or qandi or khanda?

The word candy stems from the Indian Sanskrit *khanda* meaning "piece of sugar' and Arabic *qandi* meaning "sugared." Did you know that people from India were the first to begin sucking the sweet juice from the tall thick grass there called sugarcane?

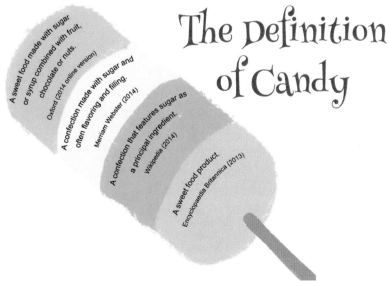

A sweet food made with sugar or syrup combined with fruit, chocolate or nuts.
Oxford (2014 online version)

A confection made with sugar and often flavoring and filling.
Merriam Webster (2014)

A confection that features sugar as a principal ingredient.
Wikipedia (2014)

A sweet food product.
Encyclopaedia Britannica (2013)

The Definition of Candy

Using four common sources below, candy is often defined as something with sugar either as the main ingredient or combined with….well... something. Of course, we are already getting ourselves in trouble here given that sugar is not the main ingredient in "candied" fruit slices nor is sugar the main ingredient in chocolate, and don't even get us started on gum. Encyclopedia Britannica cleared the mystery up a bit for us when it states that the term candy means something different in other countries with chocolate considered candy in the US but not elsewhere. Interestingly, other countries separate their confections into chocolate confections, sugar-based confections and starch-based confections. Since we US Americans love our chocolate so much, we'll include it in our candy story.

Of course, two paragraphs later, Encyclopedia Britannica confuses us again when they argue, similar to Wikipedia, that sugar is the main ingredient in candy. Huh? Oh wait, they say sugar is the main ingredient for most candy. Ok, so chocolate, candied fruit and gum is not most candy (or are they?). Are you spinning yet? We are! And, to really get your head really twirling, candy can still be candy when not made with (white) table sugar, aka sucrose. Candy can be made with any sweetener like honey, molasses,maple syrup, corn syrup, or even artificial sweeteners. Heck, it was only in this millennium that candy was made with actual sugar.

So, where does that leave us with our original question: *What is candy?* Well, we know it's sweet, and candy does not need sugar as a main ingredient since candy can be made with honey and other sweeteners. Pastries don't count, because, well, pastries have more flour than sugar and we, US Americans, like our candy *sweet!* And chocolate is sweet (at least milk chocolate is) so chocolate is candy.

So, is candied fruit candy? If we use Wikipedia's definition (where candy is mainly sugar), candied fruit does not count as candy because it has more fruit than sugar coating. However, fruits have natural sugars. When coated with more sugar, candied fruit ends up in the category of candy. Therefore, in this story, we welcome the candied fruit. *Bienvenue!*

11

Now onto the question of gum (chewing gum). *Is gum candy?* According to our four sources above, NO! So, why is it in this book you ask? In an impromptu survey on *Facebook* by Candy.com, over 125,000 people were asked the same question: Is gum candy?* The answer? Well, let's just say there was no consensus. Of the 86 answers we received, 23 said: *Yes, it's candy*, 35 said: *No*, and the rest said: *I don't know*. How's that for mixed feelings?

So are we adding gum to this book? Yes. Why? Because:

1. There's no consensus of whether gum is candy or not
2. If you walk into the candy aisle of any US store, you will see gum
3. It's our book and we want to.

We started this lil' candy chapter with what we thought would be a simple question: *What is candy?* (oh, how foolish we were only just a couple of pages ago). At this point, we have a slightly more sophisti-ma-cated understanding of candy. Yeah, we're still confused, but with more facts.

Anyway, what's clear is that *most* candy is *sweet*.

So, what makes candy sweet? We know this is a dumb question but follow along with us, it will make slightly more sense as we get further along this twisty, twirly, story.

Sweetness comes from a variety of sources including honey, which is considered an animal product (weird, eh?); maple syrup (resin from maple trees); fruit (e.g., dates, coconut, honeydew and almost all fruit); berries, starches and most importantly for our purposes, *sugar* (sucrose) extracted from—get this—GREENS! Hey, it's time to let your family and friends know you do eat your greens. Yup, sugar comes from grass (sugarcane); trees (palm, birch and maple); and plants (sugar beet and agave). You see, all plants have sucrose deep within them but extracting the sucrose out of vegetation is extremely hard. Sugarcane and sugar beets have the highest amount of sucrose making these two sugar sources the sweetest and most valuable. We'll talk more about where these two important sugars come from in our next chapter.

Now without further ado, let's introduce our candy family. First off is the hard candies we all know and love (at least those of us with teeth). Second, are the chocolate triplets: dark, milk, and white (Story of Goldilocks and 3 bears will help us here). Third off are the tongue-slappin' lollies (who slap in more ways than one). And last are the trees and fuel-stemmed chewing gum (which you'll probably spit out when you're done reading, in more ways than one). For this sake of a sequel, we'll leave taffy, gummies, and all the other sweets (or sours *warheads*) for later.

Note—90% of those surveyed are from the US making this survey only telling of what a small percentage of people who follow a Facebook candy page think about gum. Yes, kinda biased but interesting nonetheless.

Fruit drops:

- 1 lb. white sugar
- 4 oz powdered glucose
- 6 oz of water
- 1 teaspoon cream of tartar
- A few drops of fruit extract (essence) or flavoring oil – try pear, strawberry, peach, apricot, orange, lemon, blackcurrant, mango, etc.
- Icing sugar (confectioner's sugar), for dusting

Directions

1. In medium saucepan, stir sugar, glucose, and water together. Cook stirring, over medium heat until sugar dissolves, cover then bring to a boil. Without stirring, heat to 300-310 degrees or until a small amount of syrup dropped into cold water forms hard, brittle threads.

2. Add cream of tartar and fruit extract. Mix through quickly.

3. Pour the candy syrup into pan and leave until candy is cool enough to touch. Use scissors and cut small pieces and shape into small balls.

4. Coat with confectionery sugar. Store in airtight container.

Candy Word Scramble

1. coleoctah
2. ycnda
3. ffyat
4. egfud
5. jearkrsbeaw
6. iptrpeenmp
7. amearlc
8. eabnylesjl
9. ackoyrncd
10. oemlrnopds
11. oosplillp
12. mgu
13. caotctondny
14. lmslsahwram
15. cfhreuwist

Answers to puzzles at end of book

Chapter 2

Where did candy start?

Life can be bittersweet, but only you control the sugar. --Michelle Parsons

This chapter is about the origins of candy in the US. Or at least that is how we started. Figuring out how and when it began is just as sticky as defining what is candy. You see, people have been making candy in their homes since the time of the ancient Egyptians. You might have seen pictures of Cleopatra and her beloved honey balls (see below). In the Roman cities of the time, *dulcia* or candy was sold in candy shops and recipes were available for making dulcia at home: dates stuffed with nuts and soaked in honey.

As traders and knights of the Middle Ages came back from the Crusades, only the wealthy could afford to become sweet on sugar. At first, candy was used as medicine and later as a spice to hide the taste of rancid food (yuk) and later as a preservative for fruits creating jellies and jams. From the Middle Ages and even now, English people love their sweets more than any other culture with the English royalty eating so much candy, or "sweetmeats" as they called sugar, their teeth often turned black--reminder here--*don't forget to brush your teeth after eating sweets.*

Hey, did you notice we said how much the royalty loved their candy? Well, this is where our candy story gets…well… a little bitter. We need to talk about sugar and where the sugar came from that is used to make our beloved candy. Remember in Chapter 1 we said that sugarcane and sugar beets are the main sugar used to make candy.

So, let's start with sugarcane since a lot of the sugar in our candy comes from sugarcane. We'll talk about the sugar from sugar beets in a bit. Sugarcane is a very tall, very thick grass that grows in tropical climates where water is abundant, and heat and humidity is high. Sugar cane originated in New Guinea way back in 7,000 BC and around 327 BC in India and expanded throughout the world via trade routes.

Speaking of trading, you've probably heard the stories of Christopher Columbus setting out to find quicker spice trade routes rather than going down and around Africa to get spices from India. What is less well-known is that Columbus' father-in-law, Bartolomeu Perestrello was a major overseer of sugarcane plantations in Porto Salvo and Madeira along with some other smaller islands. Christopher probably watched how his father-in law, Bart's plantations made him super rich. So, although Christopher wanted to find easier ways to get spices, he also was probably looking for places to grow sugarcane. *How do you know that*, you say? Well, because Columbus not only knew how rich one could get from sugarcane plantations from his father-in-law's adventures but on his second voyage to the New World, Christopher brought back cuttings of sugar cane from the Caribbean (from Haiti to be exact). Columbus also likely came across cocoa on his voyages, but like many, he did not recognize its value. The wealthy fell in love with sugar so much that they wanted more of it and a market quickly opened for producing more sugar.

*Side note: At this time, sweets made from sugar were not thought of as "just for kids." Nope, when royalty in Europe ate sweets from this sugar—it was considered **healthy, exotic, and classy**. Candy made from cane sugar was also likely still being made in people's homes or in fancy candy shops.*

Back to the sugar plantations: More sugar plantations meant finding more land to grow the sugar cane. The best places to grow sugarcane is in the hot and steamy tropics and so a quick race to conquer and own the tropic islands in the Caribbean happened between Spain, France and England.

The English loved their candy more than any other country in the world. So, it's no surprise to learn that the English created the largest sugar plantations in the Caribbean including in

Barbados, Jamaica, Antiqua, and Montserrat. The British loved their sugar so much that they engaged in huge naval battles with France and Spain to maintain control over the sugar-producing Caribbean islands.

So, you say, *what's the big deal? Yay, yay, yay, sugar plantations, tropics, Columbus, naval battles, Caribbean and…get to the point, already. Talk about candy, candy, candy!*

Ok, we're getting there. But first, who do you think were the workers on these labor-intensive, stifling hot, sugar plantations? It wasn't Columbus or his father-in-law or any of the royalty or even the regular people like you and me. At first, the Spanish, French and English who conquered the West Indies wanted the land to grow tobacco, cotton, and sugar and they tried to have the island natives do this back-breaking work but many of the natives knew the terrain and quickly ran away. Then, the Europeans brought in indentured slaves (often troublemakers or criminals from England, Spain and France) to do this difficult work but there were not enough of these folks. Once these indentured slaves completed their indentured time, they high-tailed it out of there as fast as they could. Did we say this was back-breaking deadly work? No one wanted to work on the sugar plantations! Finally, the

English turned to slaves, yup African slaves from the African nations of Sierra Leone, Ghana, Ivory Coast, Cameroon, Nigeria and Guinea. You see the slaves did not speak the language of their captors or islanders and had nowhere to run once on these tiny islands in the Caribbean.

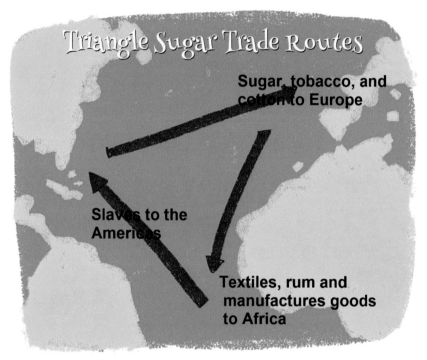

So, just how many African slaves were shipped to the Caribbean to work on these harsh sugar plantations? The British shipped around 250,000 African slaves to the Caribbean during the 16th century. In the 1700s, at the height of West Indian sugar production, the British shipped 45,000 African slaves to the Caribbean EVERY YEAR! With so much sugar being made from all these slaves, the price of sugar dropped a lot. The price dropped so much that the regular English people and others could afford to buy sugar. So much candy was being made at this time that business-minded people started to think of ways to make more candy. And this is about the time that mass-produced candy, that is, machine made candy, arrived cutting the cost of candy even more.

Sugar making on plantations from the sugarcane fields to sugar boiling
Reproduced from: Charles de Rochefort. *Histoire naturelle et morale des iles Antilles de l'amerique.* Rotterdam, A. Leers, 1665.

So, we FINALLY get to the even sadder side of the candy story: Sugar, in the form of sugarcane, since its very beginnings, has as its basic ingredient... slavery. Without slavery, sugar and most candy, would likely have been rare throughout the world. This is definitely a bitter bit of candy to swallow.

DANGER: More bitter swallowing ahead: As the price of candy dropped due to the high supply of sugar and the ability to mass produce candy, the regular people in England could now afford to buy what was once only for the rich. So, sugar allowed all the English people to be able to have candy while creating world discrimination by enslaving Africans on the sugar plantations in the Caribbean. Twisty, twirly, head hurt, eh, even more bitter than an *Atomic Warhead* or even *Toxic Waste*.

Ok, ok, you say, *I won't eat sugar, I'll have chocolate instead.* Not so fast candy-hopper. Two problems with that option:

1. Chocolate without sugar is too bitter to eat
2. Chocolate has its own bitter story.

Before, we go further, let's return to the sugar beet for a bit. Sugar beet—called *free sugar*—became an alternative to slave-produced cane sugar in the 19th century when the means for extracting the sucrose became more available. Sugar beet grows in more temperate climates where there is fertile soil and adequate rainfall. Mechanically harvested, sugar beets do not have the same nasty slave past as sugar cane. Sucrose from sugar beets still only represents about 35% of the total sucrose produced globally. The US is the third largest global producer of sucrose from sugar beets with Russia and France as the two top largest producers. Within the US, sugar beets represent 55% of sucrose produced. Yay for free sugar.

I bet you were wondering what's happening within the world of sugarcane today. *Umm, no* you say. Well you know we're gonna tell you anyway, right. ♏ So, you say, *O-K but it's has to be better now, right?* (don't you love the way we talk for you. Hehe). Well, as we, candy lovers, search for some good news in this bittersweet tale, we can hang on tight to the following facts. Sugarcane production is not as nasty as it once was during the 1600s-1800's as slavery is all but banned in much of the world. And, the US produces 90% of its own sugarcane so most US sugar workers get paid a decent wage. The rest of the

22

sugarcane used in the US is imported from 15 other countries (located in South America, Australia and South Africa) with the top five being Mexico, Brazil, Philippines, Guatemala and Dominican Republic.

Sadly, Brazil and the Dominican Republic have working conditions that resemble slavery. However, the sugarcane imported from these two countries represents less than .025% of all the sugarcane consumed within the US.

For the sake of finishing our story before you finish your lolly, we will now confine our lil' candy story to the US. However, narrowing our focus to the US still proved as messy as having gum stuck to your shoe. As many know, the Native American Indians lived in the US before the US became ..well the US. And, to complicate our story even more, the US did not officially exist until 144 years after the colonists arrived. So here was our conundrum: what historical measure should we use as the place where candy started? When we say place, do we mean candy makers across current US territory regardless of time? Or should we begin in the year of the US' official birth (1776 for anyone who didn't pass US History), including only those territories belonging to the US at that point in time?

We warned you this would get sticky. Since this is our lil' candy story, we decided on using 1776 as the starting point of candy in the US (after all, no US means no US history). All territories of the US as of 2018 will be given their dues in later chapters.

So, where was commercial candy being made and what kind of candies were being made in 1776 when the Declaration of Independence was signed? Well hold onto to your *Skittles* because candy land is about to get wild again.

In our search, we found two big names: Nicholas Bayard II who made hard candy and John Hannon who made chocolate (whether for eating or drinking, we're not quite sure).

Nicholas Bayard II

In 1730, Nicholas Bayard II from New York City opened the first sugar refinery near the current NYC stock exchange. Eventually, he owned two "sugar houses" [named "Bayard's Sugar House"] that produced refined sugar. Bayard also traded sugar for food with the Caribbeans transporting this sugar to England where the English used it to make sugar candy (later known as the penny candy circa 1830s) and then Bayard shipped his sugar candy to NYC to be sold. So loyal reader, does this sugar making count as US candy-making? And, if that little conundrum was not enough, Bayard's sugar house refined both sugar and had a sugar artisan from Europe making sugar candy for him (although it still took place in the US). At the time, Bayard advertised his "sugar-candy" for its medicinal uses (You're probably thinking "what the flubbernugget?!?" but we'll explain.)

In the ancient year of 1730 (note the sarcasm), people of all classes didn't eat foods based on vitamin or nutrient intake. Anemia was always a potential problem. It was an epidemic in the lower classes and could sometimes be found in the richer folks who were overworked or on special weight loss diets (cough *women* cough). To counteract the fainting spells and dizziness that may come with anemia, people would take sugar water or sweet lozenges. Does taking sweet lozenges for fainting spells and dizziness count as candy? Do you need a "sweet lozenge" now to deal with this dizzying candy story?

By 1776, Bayard was...well...dead. He died in 1765 to be exact, leaving his estate to his son Nicholas III (yes, another Nicholas. 1730s Bayard was Nicholas II). The business would last until 1789--through the revolution. Throughout the life of the two sugar refineries, only the wealthy could afford to buy the sugar lozenge (we are not sure whether to call this "medicinal lozenge" candy).

John Hannon--America's chocolate

In 1765, Irish immigrant, John Hannon built the first chocolate mill in Milton (a former saw mill) financed by a Dr. James Baker. Then in 1768, after the saw mill was sold, Hannon moved his chocolate business to a "fulling mill" in Dorchester, Massachusetts. What's a fulling mill, you ask (or not)? Who knows. It may have been (or is) a mill for

Old Baker's Chocolate Mill in Dorchester, MA

filling up bellies, or pastries, or pots (potbellies!), but we really doubt it. After a bit a Googling to Wikipedia, we found that fulling is the cleaning of cloth to make it thicker. What it has to do with the plot? Not much. Now back to the topic.

In 1776, Hannon was the official owner of the chocolate business, making him the first chocolatier in the U.S. Time for another fun (or not so fun) fact. In the years 1775 and 1776, a certain place named Dorchester Heights (that overlooks Boston Harbor and downtown), was used as a battleground of sorts to fight against the British and British loyalists.

How did this chocolate business survive during this tumultuous time, you ask? You probably didn't, but we will answer anyway. After the Boston Tea Party of May 10, 1773, the colonists boycotted tea and went for other beverages. The replacement? Coffee. Oh wait, and hot chocolate too. So did Hannon profit off of war? We'll let you decide.

In 1779 John Hannon died. After a battle with Hannon's wife (she wasn't the best business woman), James Baker took over the business in 1780 and built the Baker's chocolate empire that still exists today. Now, many might say Baker's chocolate is not candy nor even edible chocolate for that matter. So, maybe Baker's chocolate mill in Dorchester does not count as the birthplace of candy but Baker's company, now called *The Baker Chocolate Company* claims to be one of the first chocolate companies and if you consider chocolate to be candy then Hannon's chocolate is the origins of candy manufacturing in the US. Guess you'll have to decide if you consider Baker's chocolate to be candy. Maybe you could ask their parent company, *Kraft Foods*.

So, what is our answer to the origins of candy in the US. Well, its seems pretty clear that Nicholas Bayard was the first person to make and commercially sell hard candy in the US. Now, the chocolate story is melting intoa bit of a mess.

Did Hannon make drinking chocolate? Or did he make edible chocolate that we know today? Or did he only make ground chocolate and let the consumers decide whether to drink, bake, or eat this chocolate? Let's take a look in The Chocolate Box (if you're confused, look down...the page, not your feet).

Egyptian Honey balls (Tigernut Sweets)

Ingredients:
- 7 oz. of fresh dates (approximate)
- 1 tablespoon Cinnamon powder (to taste)
- 2 tablespoons roughly chopped walnuts
- 2 tablespoons finely ground almonds
- Honey (acacia honey if possible)
- A little water

Directions:
1. Blend the date with the water to form a rough paste.
2. Add the cinnamon (to taste) and chopped walnuts.
3. Roll the mixture into small balls.
4. Coat in honey.
5. Coat with the ground almonds and serve.

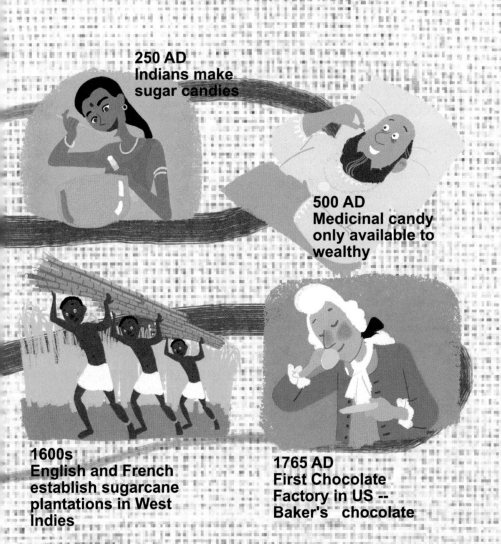

250 AD
Indians make sugar candies

500 AD
Medicinal candy only available to wealthy

1600s
English and French establish sugarcane plantations in West Indies

1765 AD
First Chocolate Factory in US -- Baker's chocolate

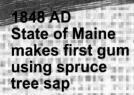

1848 AD
State of Maine makes first gum using spruce tree sap

1850s AD
380 candy factories in US and chocolate is mass produced

Candy Fill-in-the-blanks

1. In the Middle Ages only the _____ ate sweets.

2. Sugar cane originated in _____.

3. _____ brought sugar cane cuttings back from the Caribbean to Spain.

4. Spain, France and _____ had many naval battles fighting for islands in the West Indies.

5. Triangle trade routes included Caribbean, Europe and _____.

6. _____ slaves left the sugar plantations as soon as they could.

7. British shipped _____ slaves a year from Africa to Caribbean.

8. _____ had the largest sugar plantations in the Caribbean.

9. _____grow in temperate climates.

10. The first sugar refinery house in the US was started by _____.

Answer key at end of book

Chapter 3

Let's open the chocolate box:
Three shades of chocolate heaven

Mama always said, life was like a box of chocolates. You never know what you're gonna get. - Tom Hanks (from the film *Forrest Gump*, 1994)

Ahh, *cho-co-late*, food of the gods.

Originally chocolate came from the forests of South America where the Mayans and Aztecs roasted the beans from the cacao tree, then they would grind the beans and mix with peppers, chilis and flowers making a spicy drink called *Xacoatl*. This amazing concoction was only drunk by royalty as the cacao beans were so valuable they were used in place of money: Alex Teich, expert on Aztec trading culture in Azteck Trading Culture reports that 3 cacao beans were worth an avocado or a fish wrapped in maize husks.

NOTE: Cacao vs. Cocoa. They're different. Cacao is the beans released from the pods while cocoa is the powder that is produced when cocoa is processed with high heat. Sometimes cocoa butter is added to cocoa during the high heat process.

WHAT IS IT WORTH?

Turkey Hen — 100 beans

Rabbit — 100 beans

Small rabbit —30 beans

Turkey egg —3 beans

Avocado —3 beans

Large tomato—1 beans

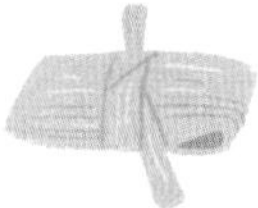

Tamale —1 beans

Cactus fruit — 1 beans

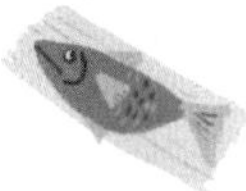

Fish wrapped in maize husks — 3 beans

Chopped firewood —1 beans

5 chiles — 1 beans

Spanish explorer Hernan Cortes brought cocoa back to Spain where it was kept a secret for 100 years and only the royalty drank it. See a pattern here, non-royal, readers? It is only when a Spanish and French (King Louis XIV of France) royal wedding occurred that the public learned of cocoa that Europe fell in love with chocolate. By the 17th century, hot chocolate became fashionable in London and in true British "love of sweets" form, the spices and bitterness of *Xacoatl* was replaced with milk and sugar. Remember from earlier chapters that sugar was available in Europe by this time. The Catholic Church regarded cocoa as so sacred that it was exempt during a fast—Cocoa was truly blessed by the church.

Warning: Bitter side of chocolate story ahead. Sadly, chocolate has a bittersweet history similar to sugarcane's history. Cocoa grows best in hot humid climates similar to sugarcane. As the demand for cocoa increased, British, Dutch and French ships went to the islands off Portugal and to Western African countries, especially Ghana and the Ivory Coast where cocoa plantations were established. Producing cocoa was dangerous, slow and hard work and from the 17th through the 19th century, it was all done by hand.

With the industrial revolution, some machinery became available to use in cocoa production on the plantations and in chocolate making production. Chocolate evolved into all shapes, forms, and derivatives. And by derivatives, we mean

dark chocolate, milk chocolate, and white chocolate. What's the difference between dark, milk and white chocolate? Well, it has everything to do with the cocoa solids and cocoa fats. To understand these three cocoa, we'll use the Goldilocks' story with Papa bear, Mama bear, and Baby bear as our chocolate stars. If you get the metaphor, kudos to you. Now onward.

Side note: Today, two-thirds of the cocoa in the world comes from West Africa where cocoa farmers work 12-14 hours a day and earn $2/day—well below poverty. So, many cocoa plantation owners use child labor to keep their costs low. Much of cocoa production is still done by hand. Lawmakers in the US are putting pressure on the chocolate industry to certify that their chocolate is child-labor free. Let's hope they succeed so we can enjoy our chocolate, guilt free.

Papa Bear (Dark Chocolate)

In our last chapter, we left off at the mystery that is *Hannon's Best Chocolate* (that's the name Hannon gave his chocolate product, in case anyone's was wondering).

James Baker

Most likely, Hannon's chocolate product was used to make hot chocolate or some other chocolate beverage. According to the Bostonian Society's website, while only financing Hannon's chocolate business in 1765, in 1772, Dr. James Baker also helped *ground* the chocolate. It was not until 1866, that Walter Baker began using a Van Houten cocoa-butter press--the same year that Cadbury began using its first press to increase chocolate production. So, what was happening between 1765 and 1866, you might ask. Well, mostly people were buying powdered chocolate to bake and make hot chocolate drinks. Ironically, the machines that the Baker's chocolate company and other companies were using during this period pulled the cocoa-butter out (as fat does not taste good in hot chocolate drinks) and considered it waste. Cocoa powder is quite bitter and was mixed with water, milk and other spices into a delicious hot drink. Sounds like a liquified chocolate bar to us.

According to Samira Kawash in her book, *Candy: A Century of Panic and Pleasure*, the only chocolate available

up until 1845 was coarse and bitter and only suitable for cooking and drinking rather than for candy. Tim Richardson in his book, *Sweets: A History of Candy*, marks 1847 as the first time a chocolate bar was produced that was for eating and not baking or drinking.

Who were these chocolate bar pioneers? There was *Lindt* in Switzerland, *Fry* in Bristol, and *Caffarel* in Italy. Fry's and Sons are credited with developing the first edible chocolate outside of ground chocolate used for baking and hot cocoa (Bostonian Society, 2005). *Cadbury* followed (and subsequently merged with and took over) Fry and others in testing out this new product. At first, there was little interest in this new type of chocolate by consumers and manufacturers with drinking chocolate continuing to outsell eating chocolate well into the 21st century. This lag in sales may in part have been due to the gritty texture of the "edible" chocolate.

Moving away from the European tour, in 1849, Walter Baker, grandson of James Baker of the eventual *Baker's Chocolate* empire (now part of *Krafts*), introduced eating chocolate to the US in the form of *Caracas Sweet Chocolate*. In the same year, Baker's established trade relations with San Francisco, California.

So, the papa bear of chocolate is dark chocolate considered by many chocolate connoisseurs as the *only* real chocolate worthy of eating. Using statistics based on chocolate consumption, 35% of chocolate lovers prefer dark chocolate while a whooping 51% percent prefer milk chocolate and only 8% prefer white chocolate*. Let's turn now to the most favored chocolate of all--milk chocolate.

Side note: Data on chocolate consumption is from 2012 representing % of preference.

Mind Bender: Can you figure out why we chose milk chocolate as the baby bear of chocolate?

Boxed Chocolates

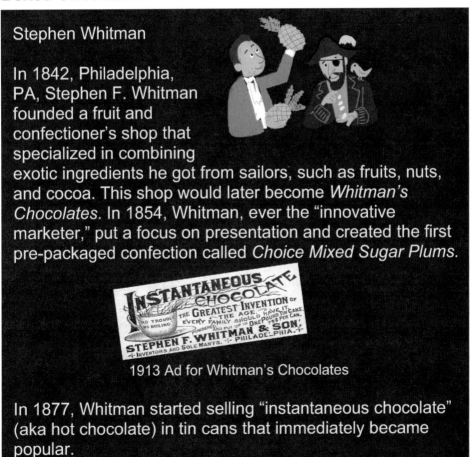

Stephen Whitman

In 1842, Philadelphia, PA, Stephen F. Whitman founded a fruit and confectioner's shop that specialized in combining exotic ingredients he got from sailors, such as fruits, nuts, and cocoa. This shop would later become *Whitman's Chocolates*. In 1854, Whitman, ever the "innovative marketer," put a focus on presentation and created the first pre-packaged confection called *Choice Mixed Sugar Plums*.

1913 Ad for Whitman's Chocolates

In 1877, Whitman started selling "instantaneous chocolate" (aka hot chocolate) in tin cans that immediately became popular.

By 1907, Walter P. Sharp from *Whitman and sons, Inc.* created the first sampler box. In case anyone doesn't know, a sampler box is a small box containing an assortment of a company's best-selling chocolate. Milk chocolate made its appearance in the sampler by 1984 and sugar-free chocolate in 2001.

It is now tradition that American presidents offer *Whitman Samplers* to White house guests and those traveling on Air Force One. *Lindt* now owns the *Whitman Sampler.*

Domingo Ghirardelli

In California, Italian-born Domingo Ghirardelli who spent a considerable amount of time in Uruguay and Peru, paved the way to eventual chocolate glory. Hearing of the gold rush and urged on by his former neighbor James Lick (who eventually died the richest man in California), Ghirardelli relocated to the US, failed to find gold, and opened a shop selling supplies and confections to miners. Within months, he opened a second shop located at the corner of Broadway and Battery streets in San Francisco. In 1851, a fire that destroyed a fifth of San Francisco took down Ghirardelli's business.

Ghirardelli quickly opened a *Cairo's Coffee House*, but this business failed, and he eventually moved back into the confectionary business. In 1852, he founded *Ghirardlly & Girard*, which would later become the *Ghirardelli* owned by *Lindt* (Yep. You read that right) that we know today.

Russell Stover

The next giant in the US boxed chocolate empire came in 1923 in the form of Russell and Clara Stover of Denver, CO (*Russell Stover*, 2015).

Baby Bear (Milk Chocolate)

Twenty-eight years after the first dark chocolate bar was created, a former candle maker in Switzerland named Daniel Peter created the first milk chocolate. In 1875, with the help of the milk powder formula by his neighbor Henri Nestlé (1814-1890) (who would eventually start the *Nestle's* company), Peter created a new chocolate bar named *Gala* (meaning "from the milk"). In 1878, Peter exhibited his chocolate bar at the Paris International Exhibition winning 2nd place.

But when does milk chocolate reach the good ole' (albeit still young in those days) US of A, you ask.

Well, Swiss milk chocolate traversed the Atlantic Ocean in the form of *Peter's Chocolate* of the *Peter, Cailler, Kohler Company*, entering the US in 1908 by way of... let the drumrolls begin... NYC (surprise, surprise). The first Swiss milk chocolate company to enter the US would later merge with present-day giant *Nestlé* (who also came to the US to sell condensed milk, chocolate and coffee) in 1929 (which is also the first year of the Great Depression, mind you).

By 1951, *Nestle* owned *Peter's Chocolate* by way of *Lamant, Cortiss and Company* (Henri Nestle's early company) and in 2002, Peter's brand was bought by *Cargill* who still owns the company today. In the 1950's, *Nestle* also distinguished itself with one of the most memorable jingles of all time: *'N-E-S-T-L-E-S, Nestle's makes the very best chocolate."*

Oh yeah and we cannot forget the quintessential American chocolate candy bar *Hershey*. In 1900, as with all things American, Milton Hershey commercialized milk chocolate candy bars using fresh milk. We think Milton was trying to make his *Hershey* bars different from *Nestle'* who was using condensed milk for their chocolate bars.

In typical capitalist fashion, these chocolate makers began buying up smaller candy companies, becoming some of the largest businesses in the world today. Their values are estimated to be in the billions—all from the little cocoa bean. For example, Hershey is currently owned by the *Hershey Trust Company* and is estimated by Forbes magazine to be worth $22.3 billion aka $23,300,000,000. That's a lot of zeros! Of course, *Hershey*'s makes and sells much more than Hershey chocolate bars now, as does *Nestle* and other commercialized candy making giants. Given that the chocolate industry is predicted (2018) to reach 98.3 BILLION dollars, *Hershey* owns a significant share of the chocoholic's sweet tooth. Amazingly, *Mars* eclipses *Hershey* with three times the value. Why? Well, mainly because they have the TOP two biggest selling candy bars in the world. Any ideas on the number one and two top selling candy bar every year since their debut?

Candy Trivia: Guess who are the top three candy makers in the world?

Hint: These 3 companies have access to ALL the resources needed to make their own chocolate and two have their own cocoa plantations. ...

Answer: *Nestle*' is the largest candy company in in the world; followed by *Mars* which is stilled family-owned; and in third place is *Hershey*. Maybe *Nestle*' and *Mars* are one and two because they own their own cocoa plantations around the world. Sweet, ey.

Company	Top Candy Items	Net Sales 2017 (US$ millions)
Mars Wrigley Confectionery, div of Mars Inc (USA)	Snickers, Mars, Skittles, Dove, and M&Ms	18,000
Mondelēz International (USA)	Cadbury, Toblerone	11,560
Ferrero Group (Luxembourg / Italy)	Ferrero Roche, Tic Tacs, Lemonheads, Redhots	12,000
Nestlé SA (Switzerland)	Baby Ruth, 100 Grand Bar, Wonka candy, Butterfinger	8,818
Meiji Co Ltd (Japan)	Meiji	9,652
Hershey Co (USA)	Hershey's, Reese's, Almond Joy, Kit Kat, Jolly Rancher, Kisses, Mounds	7,533
Chocoladenfabriken Lindt & Sprüngli AG (Switzerland)	Lindt, Ghirardelli, Whitman, Russell Stover	4,106
Arcor (Argentina)	Arcor blow-up candy, fruit filled candy, Menthol Plus, Butter Toffees, Bon o Bon	3,100
Ezaki Glico Co Ltd (Japan)	Pocky	3,242
Pladis (UK)		2,816

Candy Industry, January 2018 * This includes production of non-confectionery items

Mama Bear (White Chocolate)

White chocolate, the mama of the chocolate family arrived in 1930. According to websites *Chocolate Wrappers* and *The Nibble*, like dark and milk chocolate, white chocolate was conceived in Switzerland, by *Nestlé*. The first white chocolate bar appeared in 1936 and was called the *Galak* bar while the first US mass-produced white chocolate was the *Alpine White bar* (white chocolate with almonds) in 1948 and discontinued in 1990s.

So why do some chocolate critics argue that Mama White chocolate isn't really part of the chocolate family. Well, this is because white chocolate is pure cocoa butter, no cocoa powder or milk added. Originally, white chocolate was made as a way to use the excess cocoa butter created while making dark and milk chocolate. Sounds like chocolate to us, creamy, yummy, fat-filled, calorie-rich, chocolate. What do you think? Is white chocolate, really chocolate?

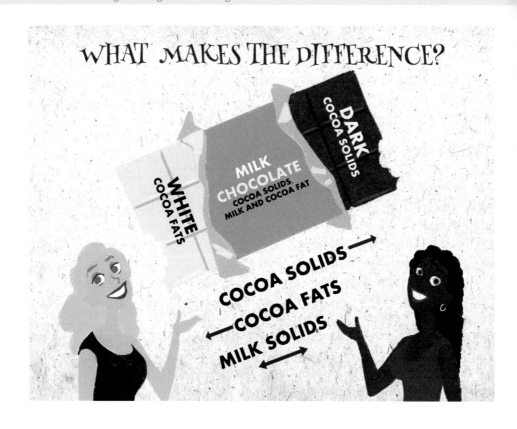

WHAT MAKES THE DIFFERENCE?

Salted Chocolate Caramel a and Pecan Turtle Clusters

Ingredients

- 2-½ cups pecans

For Caramel:
- ½ cup butter
- 1 cup brown sugar
- pinch of salt
- ¼ cup honey
- 7 oz sweetened condensed milk (half of a can)
- ½ teaspoon vanilla

44

Chocolate Candy Bar Matching

Can you match the candy bar with their ingredients? Match the letter beside the candy bar.

	Candy Bar	Ingredients	
	Snickers	a.	Dark chocolate, coconut
	Mars	b.	Milk chocolate, wafer, creme
	Milky Way	c.	Milk chocolate, peanut butter crisp
	3 Musketeers	d.	Milk chocolate, peanuts
	Reeses Peanut butter	e.	Milk chocolate, crisped rice
	Mounds	f.	Milk chocolate, cookie, caramel
	Almond Joy	g.	Milk chocolate, peanuts, caramel
	Kit Kat	h.	Milk chocolate, peanuts, caramel, nougat
	Hershey's Bar	i.	milk chocolate, nougat, whipped chocolate
	Butterfinger	j.	Chocolate, peanuts, caramel, fudge
	Heath	k.	Milk chocolate, crispy rice
	Nestle's Crunch	l.	milk chocolate, chocolate nougat, caramel
	Pay Day	m.	Milk chocolate, peanut butter
	Mr. Goodbar	n.	Milk chocolate, nougat, almonds, caramel
	Clark bar	o.	Chocolate, toffee
	Twix	p.	Milk chocolate, coconut, almonds
	Baby Ruth	q.	Milk chocolate, peanuts, caramel, nougat
	Oh Henry	r.	Milk chocolate
	100 Grand	s.	Milk chocolate, peanuts, caramel
	Krackel	t.	Chocolate, peanut butter crisp

Answer Key for candy bar matching at end of book

The Art of Chocolate Making

The Art of Chocolate Making

According to Ecole Chocolat's website ChocoMap.com, there are eight steps to making chocolate from cacao. We'll describe it loosely here.

1. Harvest the cacao seeds/pods/beans (or however you want to call it) and ferment for about eight days. We'll note that cacao trees grow in subtropical areas like Central and South America and Africa. The cacao pods are still hand-picked today (*child labor* cough *human trafficking* cough *slavery* cough). We'll talk about it by book's end.

2. Dry the cacao.

3. Roast from ten to thirty-five minutes.

4. Push the cacao on a journey through serrated cones (or other obstacles) and crack them, separating the cacao shell and kernel to create *cocoa nibs*.

5. Blow the nibs to completely divorce the brittle shells from the kernels.

6. Grind and roll the nibs until the cacao butter is released creating a chocolate liquid.

7. Conch or knead the cacao mixture for hours or days until it is the consistency desired depending on the type of chocolate desired.

8. Temper and pour the chocolate into molds.

History of Iconic Chocolate Candy Firsts

1800s

- 1854 **Whitman's Chocolate**
- 1868 Cadbury first Valentine's Day box of chocolates
- 1896 New York confectioner makes **Tootsie Rolls**, names after his daughter, **1900s**
- 1900 Milton Hershey **Hershey's Milk Chocolate Bar**
- 1906 **Hershey's Milk Chocolate Kisses** covered in silver foil wrap
- 1908 Hershey's **Milk Chocolate Bar with Almonds**

1910s

- 1913 **Goo Goo Clusters**

- **1920s**
- 1920 **Oh Henry! Bar**
- 1922 H.B. Reese, **Reese's Peanut Butter Cup** first peanut butter covered in Hershey's Milk Chocolate
- 1923 Curtiss Candy Co **Baby Ruth** candy bar named for Babe Ruth
- 1923 Peter Paul **Mounds Chocolate Bar,** coconut covered in milk chocolate
- 1923 Mars **Milky Way Candy Bar**, first candy with nougat center
- 1925 Hershey **Mr. Goodbar**, first Milk Chocolate Bar with Peanuts
- 1926 **Milk Duds**

- **1930s**
- 1930 M&M Mars **Snickers Bar**, named after Mars family's beloved horse
- 1931 **Tootsie Roll Pops**
- 1932 M&M Mars **3 Musketeers**, featuring chocolate, vanilla, and strawberry nougat.
- 1936 William Luden's **5th Avenue Candy Bar**
- 1938 Hershey's **Krackel Bar** includes milk chocolate and Rice Krispies
- 1939 **Hershey's Miniatures** chocolate bars
- 1939 Overland Candy Company chocolate-covered malt balls called **Giants** and later changed the name to **Whoppers**

1940s
- 1941 **M&M's Plain Chocolate candies**
- 1945 M&M Mars changes formula for **3 Musketeers Bar** to all chocolate, eliminating vanilla and strawberry flavors
- 1949 **Junior Mints**

1970s- 1990s
- 1978 Hershey's **Reese's Pieces**
- 1979 M&M Mars **Twix**

Caramel Cookie Candy Bar
- 1989 Hershey **Symphony Bar,** made with almonds, toffee, and milk chocolate
- 1992 M&M Mars **Dove Dark Chocolate Bar** and **Dove Milk Chocolate Bar.**
- 1993 Hershey **Miniature Hershey's Kisses** & white chocolate kisses **Hugs**

2000s
- **Butterfinger bites**
- **Hershey's Dipped Pretzels**
- **Oreo Chocolate Candy Bar**
- **Reese's Dipped Pretzels**

Chapter 4

"There's a sucker born every minute" [1869 David Hannum]

A history of the birth of the lollipop

You probably noticed that we subtitled this, "<u>A</u> history of the birth of the lollipop" rather than "<u>The</u> birth of the lollipop." Well, that's because there are so many "historical" versions of the origins of the lolli, almost as many as the tongue licks in a lollipop. Although the saying, *"there's a sucker born every minute"* is often attributed to the famous American circus showman P.T. Barnum, no one really knows its origins. You'll discover here why this saying might just as easily have been said by someone trying to follow the story of the lollipop.

Legend has it that the origins of lollipops (sometimes spelled lollypops) can be found on cave paintings of people licking sticks used to collect honey from beehives. Also, there's evidence that the ancient Chinese, Arabs, and Egyptians made candied fruit and nuts using honey and inserting sticks into the sweet mixture, thereby making it easier to eat. This sweet mix was originally used for preserving fruits and nuts rather than as a sweet treat.

By the 17th century, as sugar from the Caribbean became more plentiful for the English, sugar moved from simply being a medicinal base to something sweet to eat. Richardson, in his 2002 book, Sweets: *A History of Candy*, writes that the distinction between the medicinal and confectionary uses of sweets was blurred from candy's very beginnings, creating a sort of crisis for apothecaries. Richardson writes that at the time, pharmacists were quite scornful of the confectioners probably because the candyman could sell sweets to those looking for something tasty rather than something to simply cure an ill.

Chinese Candied Fruit – Tanghulu

The 16th Century physician, Tabernaemontaus, claimed this of sugar candy: "As a powder it is good for the eyes, as a smoke it is good for common colds, as flour sprinkled on wounds it heals them." Pierre Pomet continues these claims in his book *A Compleat History of Drugs* (1712) where he says "Put into the eyes in fine powder, they take way their dimness, and heal them being bloodshot, as they cleane old sores, being strew'd gently upon them." (Richardson, 2002)

As described by Henry Weatherley in his 1864 book, *A Treatise on the Art of Boiling Sugar*, the English boiled sugar and inserted sticks into the sweet treat to make eating the sugary substance less messy. This boiled sugary treat on a stick marks the beginning of the first modern sugar lollipop.

Lollipop fact

Linguists say that the term 'lolly pop' literally means 'tongue slap' (which we find hilarious) since the word for 'tongue' is 'lolly' in Northern England and 'pop' means 'slap.' The London street vendor may have coined this term when vending the sweet delight. Although this was likely a soft rather than hard treat it is still considered a

By the mid 1800s, confectioners were selling their sweets on the streets including rock, stick, lozenges, and candies all made by boiling sugar. Many of the sweet sellers were also making these sweets in their cellars.

By the time of the Civil War, hard candy was put on the tips of pencils for children. They loved the candy on a stick so much that in the early 20th century automation technology created a lollipop manufacturing industry. Who is considered the original creator of manufactured lollipops? Well, again as it seems with all of candy history, sucker origin stories abound.

In the first sweet origin version, dating back to the 1880s, Arthur Spangler, from Bryan, Ohio, was one of the first makers of chocolate to put a stick into the caramel candy he was making, probably for the same reason everyone before him did

—to avoid packaging and causing a sticky situation in customers' hands.

Around the same time as Spangler, George P. Smith of *Bradley-Smith Candy Company* in New Haven, CT decided to put a stick into the balls of caramel candy he was making. Keep your eyes out for George Smith as we will hear more about him later in this candy story.

Another candy birth legend involves the owner of the *McAviney Candy Company* who in 1905 is said to have stumbled upon the lollipop by accident. The company made boiled hard candies that were stirred with a stick, and at day's end, the owner brought the sticks covered with the candy home for his kids to enjoy. By 1908, *McAviney Candy* began to market these "used candy sticks."

In 1908, the owner of the *Racine Confectioners Machine Company* from Racine Wisconsin, introduced a machine that placed a stick into hard candy at the rate of 2,400 sticks per hour. Owners believed they could produce enough lollipops (although they weren't called that yet) in a single week to supply the nation's demand for an entire year. They were called the "all-day sucker."

And, remember George Smith from earlier, of the *Bradley Smith Company*. Well he said: "*hey, we started the lollipop!*" Smith took credit for inventing the modern version of the lollipop which he began making in 1908. Hey, anyone else noticing how 1908 shows up again and again in these candy origin stories? Well anyways, back to Smith. In 1931, Smith trademarked the term "lollipop," where legend has it that he used the name of a famous racehorse named Lolly Pop. For many candy historians, the naming and trademarking of "*candy on sticks*" as lollipops marks the origins of the lollipop. Hey, notice the word lollipop connecting back to the 17th Century phrase 'tongue slap,' remember?

Born Sucker Machine

By 1916, a Russian immigrant, Samuel Born, invented an automated process for inserting the sticks into the candy batch. And, this machine was called the *Born Sucker Machine*. Sweet name for a machine, ey. Anyway, the city of San Francisco considered this machine so creative that, in 1916, they granted him the "keys to the city."

So, there you have it. Lots of tongue lick slapper stories for the birth of the lollipop. But, don't try to say that last line five times fast--or your tongue will be slapping faster than you can lick to the center of a lollipop.

Hard candy (Family Recipe)

Ingredients:
- 2 cups water
- 4 cups sugar
- 1 teaspoon of citric acid
- 5 drops of food coloring

Directions:
1. Mix sugar and water in a pot
2. Boil the mixture to 320° Fahrenheit (use a candy thermometer to check)
3. Remove from heat
4. Add food coloring and citric acid
5. Put in mold, make small drops, or just let it cool

All things Sugar Crossword Puzzle

Across

4)   Paste made of sugar and water
6)   A sweetener that is used to make candy
7)   Russian immigrant that created first mass-produced lollipops
8)   Sanskrit stem of candy means piece of sugar
11) A lollipop made by Tootsie
13) jumbo lollipops that originally sold at circuses and fairs
15) hard candy on a stick named by inventor George Smith after his racehorse
16) Candy company that made first American candy machine for candy lozenges
18) Lollipops made by The Hershey Company
19) Another word for white or table sugar

Down

1)   Candy maker named this sweet after his daughter's nickname
2)   Soft, chew confection made with sugar and gelatin
3)   Square shaped lollipops
5)   Original name of this lollipop was Papa suckers
7)   First US sugar refiner
9)   Arabic stem of candy means sugared
10) Sweet made with sugar, corn syrup and pectin
12) A lollipop made by Spangler Company
14) Another name for lollipop
17) Pulled sugar

Answer Key for Crossword Puzzle at end of book

Lollipop History

1000's of years ago. Honey was collected by using a stick to get honey and then licking the honey stick

17th Century English boiled sugar water for candy treats and put sticks to make them easier to eat.

1908, Racine Confectionary Machinery Company introduced a machine that could put candy on the end of a stick making up to 2,400 lollipops per hour.

1908 George Smith owner of the Bradley Smith Company started making candy sticks and trademarked the term lollipop in 1931.

1905--McAviney Candy Company was stirring his hard candy mixture and would take the sticks covered in candy home to his children.

By 1908, McCaviney sticks were being marketed as "used candy sticks".

1912--Samuel Born invented machine that put the stick into the candy and called it the Born Sucker Machine to which Samuel earned the keys to the city of San Francisco.

Chapter 5

Chewing Gum: From Sap to Wax

"Flattery is like chewing gum. Enjoy it but don't swallow it."
—Hank Ketcham

Is gum candy? And, if so, why?

Note that gum's status also determines whether this piece should be posted on candy websites. After all, if it's not candy, why be here at all? Yep. We're chewing on the existential meaning of candy here.

If you want to know whether gum's candy, the answer: drum roll please…...we don't know.

You see, North American gum started out in the form of Spruce tree resin. The Native Americans introduced the chewing of resin from trees to the European settlers in the 17th to 18th century. The central American Indians used the Sapoldilla tree resin to make gum. Guess what the name for

people who tap the trees for this resin……Chicleros. Sound familiar? That's coz the sap collected from the Spaoldilla tree is called chicle. Yup, Chicle gum that is chewed all across America.

The ancient Greeks and Mayans had their own versions for gum resin as they tapped from the mastic tree that produces a sweet-smelling albeit smoky flavored gum. Mastic was used to clean teeth, freshen breath and calm the stomach. An aside to chew on (you know we always go aside), mastic means "to chew" in Greek. And, mastic gum is still very popular in Europe.

Most gum today is NOT made from tree resin 𝔪 but from paraffin wax or some weird synthetic gum bases. Today, gum manufacturers are tight lipped about their gum-based ingredients. Who wants some tree back in their gum?

Anyway, chewing along, gum rather than being made from mostly sugar, came from trees. Interesting aside here, "candy" stems from the Arabic word for sugared—"qandi." So, in the case of gum, trees: 1; candy: 0.

Let's get back to our American spruce resin gum. The first person to sell spruce resin gum commercially was John B. Curtis who developed chewing gum in the form of sticks, in 1848 Portland, ME, and sold it as "State of Maine Pure Spruce Gum." (Talk about an informative name, right?) Two years later, in 1850, he opened the *Curtis & Sons Company*, monopolizing the chewing gum industry for roughly 20 years. Within two decades, he managed to build the first brick building dedicated to chewing gum in the United States, in 1866.

Factory, Curtis & Son Company, first brick chewing gum factory built in the United States.

In circa 1850, while Curtis & Sons ran the gum industry, there was a movement to use paraffin wax as a gum base. Curtis started using paraffin wax as a gum base as an alternative to his original spruce tree gum recipe. The new recipe eventually surpassed the old Spruce recipe in customer popularity. Why? No one knows for sure. But either way, more popularity equals more money for the company. Paraffin thereby gradually replaced spruce resin. On the up side of this story, the spruce trees' is saved from decline by chewing gum fanatics.

Paraffin Wax

Discovered in the 1830s, paraffin wax is a white, odorless chemical compound extracted from petroleum. Currently, it is used as a food additive in chewing gum and is also used in "candles, wax paper, polishes, cosmetics, electrical insulators," to name a few (Encyclopedia Britannica). So, swallow, or spit?

Anyway, by the end of the Curtis monopoly, two doctors (yes, you read right. *Doctors)*, within months of each other, received patents for their own versions of gum. In July 27, 1869, Dentist Amos Tyler of Toledo, OH received the first US gum patent for his white resin (aka pine tree sap) and olive oil gum.

Water White Resin

In December 28, 1869, Physician William F. Semple of Mount Vernon (also Ohio) received a patent for his rubber, charcoal, and chalk gum.

At this point, swallowing is really discouraged. Moving along, despite the patents, neither doctors sold their gums (chewing gum, not dental gum, mind you) commercially.

Chicle Gum

Later on New York inventor Thomas Adams was introduced to the Mexican manilkara chicle a.k.a. the sapodilla tree by the exiled former president and general of Mexico (who was pretty old by that time) Antonio López de Santa Anna a.k.a. the man who recaptured the Alamo for Mexico.

Anna had hoped that Adams would use it as a replacement for rubber and help them both get rich. Chicle as rubber? Interesting…

In 1871, Thomas Adams received the first patent for a chewing gum *machine*. Using that machine, he manufactured "Adams New York No. 1" chewing gum—made with a chicle base.

Manikara Chicle

"Adams New York No. 1" was sold as small gumballs in colorful tissue paper in drug stores for "a penny apiece." *Chicle* has changed hands several times from *American Chicle* to a pharmaceutical company named *Warner-Lambert* to *Pfizer* (2000) to *Cadbury* (2003). Are you chewing on the realization that candy companies often eat or chew each other up a lot? We too. Do you need some gum now to calm your belly and nerves?

Anyways, Adams continued to use chicle when he founded Adams & Co in 1876 Manhattan, NY and made the first flavored gum in 1884. The gum, named *Blackjack*, was made using licorice, unlike today's *Blackjack* gum which is anise-flavored.

In 1888, Adams became the first person to introduce the coin operated vending machine to the US. (Note that the first vending machine in history sold *Holy Water* in Egypt. Seriously. *Holy water*.) His chicle-based gum dispensing machine made its debut in New York City's subway station. It sold Tutti-Frutti gum.

On June 3, 1899, New Jersey, the Conglomerate American Chicle Company—known as "The Chewing Gum trust"—was formed from five of the United States largest chewing gum manufacturers *Yucatan Gum, Adams Gum, Beeman's Gum, Kis-Me Gum, and S.T. Britten.* These five companies controlled 85% of the US chewing gum industry of the time.

Then the chewing, merging, and acquiring of gum companies got really crazy.

Wrigley

Last but not least in the gum world is Wrigley Gum. Jumping to Chicago, Illinois of 1891 William Wrigley Jr., founder of the famous *Wrigley Company*, started giving out 2 packages of gum as a bonus to customers who bought his baking powder products as a sales promotion. It worked like a charm. Two years later in 1893, he sold his first pack of *Juicy Fruits*.

Notice a difference? A few months later, Wrigley Jr. introduced *Wrigley's Spearmint*.

Did you ever wonder why chewing gum and baseball are so connected? Well that's because William Wrigley bought the baseball team the Chicago Cubs and renamed the baseball park Wrigley Field in 1927. Chewing aside, Wrigley is the oldest baseball park in the US National League with a current seating capacity of over 41,000. We imagine Wrigley gave lots of gum to his players to help them play ball.

Wrigley Company was led by members of the Wrigley family until 2006. And, by 2008, MARS, Incorporated owned *Wrigley* making Mars the largest maker of chewing gum in the world.

That's the end of our chewy tale of gum. Now time to search for gum and if you're adventurous you can try to make some Spruce Tree Gum.

Where's my Gum?

```
S R S H T R K O L E Y S B T R
W M J P U R L L E Y I R S I G
Y K A B E I I R A R O A Y U C
I E B D V A T D E H P C R R G
G E L E A E R Z E O C H U F P
R N O G C S I M D N Y I B Y A
G I X U I F A I I T T C D C R
L R R W P R L M Y N F L A I A
U P H O V L W S O I T E C U F
S H R L A O C R A H C R I J F
D E N T Y N E R M P T T K V I
D L R I T T U R F I T T U T N
M E B L A C K J A C K F G S X
E K N I S E R S J C K A Y J D
N H T W Y N V M V A I I N R G
```

BLACKJACK	OLIVE OIL	SPRUCE TREE
CADBURY	PARAFFIN	THOMAS ADAMS
CHALK	PFIIZER	TRIDENT
CHARCOAL	ROSIN	TUTTI FRUTTI
CHICLE	RUBBER	WRIGLEY
DENTYNE	SAPODILLA TREE	
JUICY FRUIT	SPEARMINT	

Recipe for Making

1. Find a black spruce tree (easiest to find in Northern American). Can tell it's a black spruce by its blue-green pine needles.
2. Look for cracks or splits in the tree where you'll find the hardened resin (gum)
3. Take about 6-8 big chunks or more.

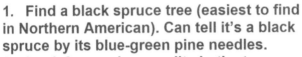

STARCH

6. Pour the gum resin into disposable straw-shaped molds. These molds can be made with aluminum foil. Be sure to squeeze end of aluminum molds so resin does not seep out.

Spruce Gum

4. Put hardened resin in a disposable (or cheap) screen on top of a pot (double boiler) stirring and cooking slowly (heat no higher than 300 degrees).

5. Gum resin will seep thru screen into pot leaving just dark bark, dirt and leaves.

YUMMY!

10. Chew immediately, give away some to friends and/or save the rest for later.

7. Put in refrigerator to cool.
8. When cool, take out of molds and coat with corn starch.
9. Cut into bite size pieces and wrap in small pieces of parchment paper. Twist ends of parchment paper to make bite-size pieces of gum.

GUM mergers, divestments and acquisitions

1983 *Leaf Group gum and candy business* acquires four gum companies (*Leaf Confectionery, Clark gum, Richarson Brands and General Mills' Donruss*). Huhtamak divests *Leaf gum* to *Damel* in 1998; *CSM* buys *Leaf* from *Huhtamaki* in 1999.

1985 Finland's gum company *Huhtamaki* acquires US *Ford Gum and Machine* and *Wuxi Leaf* in 1997

1992 *Marvel Entertainment* (yes, that comics publisher) buys *Fleer gum* and then *Canadian Concord Confections* buys

Dubble Bubble and *Fleer* from *Marvel* (another comic book company) in 1998 and acquires *Philadelphia Chewing Gum* in 2003.

1993 *Cadbury* in 1993 buys its 1st chewing gum through acquisition of Argentina gum company *Stani*, then in 2000 they buy Kraft's "Hollywood" chewing gum business and Finland's *Huhtamaki* gum company *Wuxi Leaf*, 2002 they buy *Dandy*'s gum brand; acquires 51% stake in Turkey's *Kent Gida* gum and candy business in 2002; buys *Adams* global gum division from *Pfizer* in 2003; buy remaining 49% of *Kent Gida* in 2006.

1996 *Hershey* takes over production of *Bazooka* gum from *Topps* and acquires *Leaf's gum* brands in 1996; buys *Fruit Strip and Bubble Yum* gum brands and mints from *Nabisco* in 2000; sells *Fruit Stripe, Rain-Blo & Super Bubble* gum brands to US *Farley & Sather's Candy* in 2003

2003 Ireland's *Zed Gum* acquires Leaf from *CSM*

2004 *Tootsie Roll Industries* acquires *Canada's Concord Confections*

2005 *Wrigley Company* acquires *Life Savers* and *Altoids* from Kraft food in 2005.

2008 *Mars* purchases *Wrigley* in 2008 and merges *Wrigley* into new subsidiary called *Mars Wrigley Confectionery* in 2016

Homemade Chicle Gum

- Chicle gum base (from Glee Gum)
- Sweetener (Cornstarch or Powdered sugar)
- Wax paper
- Disposable glass container (will be ruined so don't use a favorite)
- Disposable utensil (again, it will not survive)
- Pot with water
- Flavoring (vanilla extract, strawberry extract, etc.)
- Citric acid if using fruit flavoring

Step 1: Put chicle base in jar (enough to reach 1/4 of the jar) and put jar into the pot of boiling water, making sure the water does not get into the jar. Boil the water for about 20 minutes until *Chicle* is melted. Stir frequently.
Step 2: Mix in a few drops of flavoring (and citric acid if fruit flavored)
Step 3: Pour powdered sugar (or cornstarch) onto wax paper. Remove the chicle from jar and knead on wax paper. Step 4: Cut into pieces and serve. Wrap extras in wax paper.

Chapter 6

Fluctuating candy love: Good, bad or just misunderstood

"A spoonful of sugar helps the medicine go down."
--Name of song in Disney movie Mary Poppins.

What are some things learned on our lil' twirly tale of candy? Well, that there's some bitterness and health concerns with plenty of confusion, zaniness galore and mad, mad, love for candy.

Candy companies should NOT buy or use child-labor for their chocolate. Period !

If you have diabetes or someone in your family has diabetes, then EAT LESS SUGAR. And BRUSH YOUR TEETH after you eat candy. You don't want to be like Queen Elizabeth the 1st whose teeth turned black from eating so much candy *she didn't brush.*

All candy lovers need to remember the story of *Goldilocks and the Three Bears*. Recall, that the best bed was the one that is not too hard or not too soft, the best porridge was the one that's not too cold or too hot. What was just right for baby bear was always right in the middle. MODERATION! Not too much and not too little!

Boy, oh boy is candy misunderstood starting with what is candy, when and where did candy begin, and whether gum is candy—oh no, we're starting to twirl again.

Just one more twirl—we can't resist. What's the difference between dessert and candy? Not much really, since dessert usually has about the same amount of sugar as your favorite candy bar. Non- sweet desserts don't really taste like, well, a dessert if they are not sweet, right?!? Desserts literally means the sweet course at the end of a meal. And, then there are those granola and energy bars that people eat. They often have as much sugar as a Kit Kat. Yup, adults are eating a lot of candy too but in repackaged candy marketing ploys—called granola and energy bars.

The candy world has ALOT of colorful characters, stories and adventures as crazy and weird as WILLY WONKA, IDAHO SPUD or WHATCHAMACHALIT. Oh, and we learned that the favorite candy bars of all time are loaded with peanuts and milk chocolate.

Candy makes people happy, it can bring a smile to someone's face and it has the amazing ability—through smell and taste—to remind people of the good times. And, candy can brighten up a bad day. No food, toy or flower can match how quickly candy can change someone's mood…for the better!

That's all for now candy lovers. Do you have ideas for the next great candy? Check out the resources (at the end of the book to send us your ideas. We'd love to hear about or see your fun, zany, and sweet candy creations. Stay sweet ever after, fellow candy lover!!

Answer Key

Chapter 1

Candy Word Scramble

1. Chocolate
2. Candy
3. Taffy
4. Fudge
5. Jawbreaker
6. Peppermint
7. Caramel
8. Jelly beans
9. Rock candy
10. Lemon drops
11. Lollipops
12. Gum
13. Cotton candy
14. Marshmallow
15. Fruit chews

Chapter 2

Candy Fill in the blanks

1. Wealthy
2. Guinea
3. Columbus
4. England
5. Africa
6. Indentured
7. 45,000
8. England
9. Sugar cane
10. Baynard

Chapter 3

Chocolate Candy Bar Matching

Candy Name		Answer
1.	Snickers	s
2.	Mars	n
3.	Milky Way	l
4.	3 Musketeers	i
5.	Reeses peanut butter cups	m
6.	Mounds	a
7.	Almond Joy	p
8.	Kit Kat	b
9.	Hershey's bar	r
10.	Butterfinger	c
11.	Heath	o
12.	Nestle's Crunch	e
13.	Pay Day	g
14.	Mr. Goodbar	d
15.	Clark bar	t
16.	Twix	f
17.	Baby Ruth	h
18.	Oh Henry	j
19.	100 Grand	q
20.	Krackel	k

All things Sugar Crossword Puzzle

Across

4   FONDANT
6   MOLASSES
7   BORN
8   KHANDA
11 CHARMSBLOW
13 WHIRLYPOPS
15 LOLLIPOP
16 NEECO
18 JOLLYRANCHER
19 SUCROSE

Down

1   TOOTSIE
2   MARSHMALLOW
3   DUMDUMS
5   SUGARDADDY
7   BAYNARD
9   QANDI
10 JELLYBEANS
12 WHISTLE
14 SUCKER
17 TAFFY

More candy information

Do you have ideas for the next great candy? Share your ideas with us @lilcandyhistory or our Instagram or Facebook page @lilcandystory. We'd love to hear about or see your fun, zany, and sweet candy creations.

Websites
www.candy.com Where you can buy all things candy
www.candyhistory.net Extensive history of candy
www.candyusa.org National candy association website
www.foodispower.org Loads of information on food justice by the Food Empowerment Project
www.chocophile.com Detailed information for the complete chocolate lover
www.chewinggumfacts.com Detailed information on chewing gum history
www.hersheycompany.com History of Milton Hershey company
www.justborn.com History of marshmallow Peeps candy company
www.nestle.com History of the largest candy company in the world
www.russelstover.com Historical timeline of Whitman and Russel Stover's chocolate
www.sweetnostalgia.com Alphabetical list of old time candy
www.mars.com History of the largest family-owned candy company in the world

Books
Hopkins, Kate. *Sweet Tooth: The Bittersweet history of candy*. NY: St. Martin's Press. 2012.
Kawash, Samira. *Candy: A Century of panic and pleasure*. NY: Faber and Faber. 2013.
Richardson, Tim. *Sweets: A History of candy*. NY: Bloombury. 2002
Simon, Charnon. *Milton Hershey: Chocolate king, Town builder*. Chicago, Children's Press. 1998.
Swain, Ruth Freeman. *How Sweet It Is (and Was): The History of candy*. NY: Holiday House. 2003.
Wardjaw, Lee. *Bubblemania: A Chewy history of bubble gum*. NY: Aladdin Paperbacks, 1997.

Credits
Products may have been mentioned without their registered trademark.

See if you can find Candy Girl

Made in the USA
Middletown, DE
05 April 2021